STÉPHANE GARNIER lives on a houseboat in Lyon with his cat, Ziggy. Ziggy is fond of humans and keen to help them learn how to be a little more like cats. He hopes you enjoy this book.

STÉPHANE GARNIER

HOW TO LIVE
LIKE YOUR CAT

*Translated from the French
by Roland Glasser*

4th ESTATE • London

4th Estate
An imprint of HarperCollins*Publishers*
1 London Bridge Street
London SE1 9GF
www.4thEstate.co.uk

First published in Great Britain in 2017 by 4th Estate
This 4th Estate paperback edition published in 2018

4

Copyright © Stéphane Garnier 2017
English translation © Roland Glasser

Stéphane Garnier asserts the moral right to be identified
as the author of this work in accordance with the
Copyright, Designs and Patents Act 1988

A catalogue record for this book
is available from the British Library

ISBN 978-0-00-827680-5

Printed and bound in Great Britain by
CPI Group (UK) Ltd, Croydon

MIX
Paper from
responsible sources
FSC
www.fsc.org
FSC® C007454

This book is produced from independently certified FSC paper
to ensure responsible forest management

For more information visit: www.harpercollins.co.uk/green

To Ziggy,
my cat

CONTENTS

CONTENTS

HOW TO LIVE
LIKE YOUR CAT

FOREWORD

Some days, you don't feel like going to work, watching the news, taking every catastrophe to heart or even caring about your own future. You don't feel like having an opinion on the government's latest reforms which make you gnash your teeth, any more than you feel like worrying over your career trajectory, or knowing if you'll have much of a pension by the time you retire.

You don't want to be constantly plagued by your own personal problems, which are themselves linked to those of your family and friends, and you don't want to fret about the quality of your diet, or feel guilty for 'destroying the planet' every time you draw a bath.

You long to switch off and unplug from it all, just for a day, just for a moment, and breathe.

I look round to see that Ziggy, my cat, has padded silently into my study. He stares at me, blinking, then leaps onto my desk and lies down on the keyboard. It's a little ritual that we've had for years now, stretching back to when I still did much of my writing in long-hand and he used to bite the cap of my pen. It makes me laugh, this game we play. It's as if on the one hand he loves that I write, but on the other hand he does all he can to prevent me writing.

Up until this moment, I considered his soft pawing at me, his comings and goings between my lap and the keyboard, to be nothing more than affectionate games. But perhaps he's been trying to tell me something else all these years, something as simple as: 'Hey, don't you feel like downing tools for the day?'

Down tools. As he nuzzles his nose into my neck, I realise that, today, I don't care if I'll be able to pay the bills, or whether the stock market is about to crash. After all, does he care?

Maybe this is the secret he's been wanting to communicate all this time: know how to let go, focus on the essentials, think about your wellbeing, be like him. Live like your cat!

Cats clearly live much better than we do. So why not follow their example?

This I did, by decoding how they operate, their aspirations and lifestyle. It had been there right in front of me, all these years, without me realising.

We have everything to learn from cats, in both our personal and our professional lives.

I invite you to discover their simple secrets, so you can take a step back from your everyday, find your wellbeing again, and smile.

But what do cats do right? How should we take inspiration from them?

From this day forward, imagine another way of viewing life, by living like your cat.

YOUR FRIEND, THE CAT

'What greater gift than the love of a cat?'

CHARLES DICKENS

Cats have fascinated us since time immemorial. We have observed them and attempted to understand their strengths, their qualities, their behaviours, their habits and their compulsions. There is a kind of magic in their ability to live serenely and to be happy – assets that cats naturally possess, and which we can certainly use in our everyday lives, both personal and professional.

Cats follow a philosophy of life that could be summed up in a few words: eat, play, sleep, look out for their comfort, and do only that which pleases them. That's already a lot compared with us. But there is much more, as you will see.

Cats have a lifestyle that allows them to live without stress, for cats have a single priority: their wellbeing. By bringing ourselves closer to their way of living, we can open up a fresh perspective, a new world view, while gaining a different, deeper understanding of ourselves.

So welcome to the cats' world view, their thoughts and their philosophy. Learn to appreciate life as they do.

YOUR CAT IS FREE

'I am the Cat who walks by himself,
and I wish to come into your cave'
RUDYARD KIPLING, *JUST SO STORIES*

Freedom, cherished freedom. Who hasn't dreamed of making freedom the driving force of their life?

Freedom to come and go, freedom to do only that which pleases you, freedom of action, freedom to follow your whims and heart's desires, freedom to be as free in your mind as you are in your body. Freedom!

Paradoxically, we all have a propensity to hobble ourselves again and again, to shackle ourselves, be it to bank loans that oblige us to work ever harder, to futile objects that seem so precious in our eyes, to habits that have turned into obligations we no longer even see, or to toxic people we force ourselves to make time for.

Perhaps the moment has come to free yourself of these shackles.

Why not try to retain only that which you love, to preserve those relationships which please you, to perform only those activities you enjoy, and to work solely at jobs that fulfil you? Heed only your own counsel, and pursue your true desires.

A lovely fantasy, you might think. Not for cats, who have chosen to be free, to have what they like, be what they like, and live how they like every moment of their lives. Freedom is a constant for cats; it's much more than second nature. Being free is the very heart of their lives. The rest matters little to them in the end, whereas we often relegate this ideal to booking some time off work when our schedule allows.

You want to live like your cat? Be free as the air and do only what you have chosen to do.

YOUR CAT IS CHARISMATIC

*'God created the cat so that humans could experience
the pleasure of caressing a tiger'*
JOSEPH MÉRY

Cats don't need to meow, leap about all over the place or kick up a song and dance in order to stand out from the crowd. You can feel a cat's presence as soon as they enter the room. No fuss is required. The cat's natural charisma ensures that everyone will notice them.

A cat's discretion and personality oblige us to look in their direction every time they pad into the lounge. Classy, very classy. Who hasn't dreamed of possessing such magnetism?

What does your cat do to give off such positive vibrations and become the focus of so much admiration?

Nothing. YOUR CAT SIMPLY IS.

And that's the cat's biggest lesson: if you wish to acquire a little more animality and charisma, simply be.

Don't hide, don't lie to yourself, don't play a role, don't whirl your arms about in an attempt to mesmerise the present company. Do nothing, that's all.

Radiate your personality as if you were a transmitter, a light source. Don't waffle on during a discussion; don't hog the floor just to blow your own trumpet, you'll only bore your audience. For they will sense, subconsciously, that it's really yourself you're trying to convince or reassure through those long monologues. That's not having charisma, it's merely being omnipresent, invasive and, ultimately, oppressive.

Haven't you ever noticed that the most charismatic people – such as those actors who are said to have 'great presence' – never overdo it? Their words are as understated as their dress.

The most charismatic people are not the most extravagant. They are present, yet always show a certain restraint.

Charisma develops the more you are honest with yourself and with other people, when you accept yourself for what you are, without resorting to artifices that don't fit your deeper personality.

An attractive personality has many forms, and each of us can develop one as long as we are simply ourselves in all circumstances, just like the cat.

Radiate the space around you with your presence and charisma by being sincere, discreet, plain and true.

YOUR CAT'S DAY

🐾 Follow your cat step by step as they proceed with their daily routine: you'll feel better for it.

7.30: THE ALARM RINGS

🐾 For many people, waking up in the morning is not always easy. So clear the grogginess away by following what your cat does.

🐾 Your cat doesn't leap out of its basket like a jack-in-the-box: that's bad for both body and mood.

🐾 Cats stretch, relax, slowly open their eyes and take the time they need to wake up.

🐾 Stretch, yawn. There's no point in jolting yourself. Your cat stretches while it's still lying down, then stands, arches its back, stretches again and yawns to fully expose its canines, then sits, blinking.

🐾 I tried this. I began to imitate Ziggy. And it really is much pleasanter than leaping out of bed like a pancake being flipped before dragging yourself to the kitchen to make a cup of tea.

🐾 This phenomenon – practised by most animals – is called 'pandiculation', a reflex action that we humans too often tend to overlook. But it is so vital to a proper wake-up and to get the day off to a good start.

YOUR CAT IS CALM (MOST OF THE TIME)

'The idea of calm is a sitting cat'

JULES RENARD

S tress is the bane of our modern societies. How can we fight it? How can we channel it?

There have been many relaxation practices and techniques developed over the last few decades. It's not a very good sign, since it means that we are increasingly stressed, and that more of us are getting stressed.

Always hard at it, always on edge; anxiety builds, insomnia too, leading to physiological effects, such as high blood pressure, then burnout.

Do we really have to live so badly? How can we change things?

Observe your cat: is it ever stressed? Rarely. Your cat oozes calm and tranquillity. Your cat sits quietly, muscles relaxed, presenting no physical signs of agitation, its gaze devoid of tension.

What we sometimes call 'stress' in a cat is in fact a heightened vigilance, an alertness to potential danger, to an event that might have disturbed the calm, restful continuum of its everyday existence. A cat pricks up its ears, focuses its gaze, observes and waits. But once the cause of concern has been identified, the cat becomes calm again and lays its head back down after a few seconds.

Your cat does not cultivate stress once a situation, or danger, has passed, been avoided or dealt with. Your cat seems to let go of whatever was bothering it – disposing of any residual intellectual traces – as if the event had never occurred. That is perhaps your cat's greatest strength, and one of the keys to its majestic calm.

Your cat's life is a structured and contemplative one – with an emphasis on comfort and wellbeing – which nothing must disturb. Cats dislike major changes to their daily routine.

The only (rare) moments of stress to enter a cat's life derive from a change to this state. If an interloper enters your cat's territory, they must be swiftly chased off. If your cat's kibble is switched for a different, cheaper, less flavoursome variety, then a firm demonstration of displeasure must be made. Likewise, cats will let you know in no uncertain terms that any long and repeated absences on your part do not meet their need for love and attention.

> To maintain your inner calm
> and peace, identify the source of your
> stress, deal with the issue thoroughly,
> then let go of it for good – don't
> ruminate or brood – and
> calm will return.

Another phenomenon observed in cats, and also noted by veterinarians, is that if a cat is often stressed, the reason frequently lies with their owner.

Cats are like sponges, they feel everything. They absorb moods, but once a certain level of tension, noise and yelling has been exceeded, they can't digest it all with their usual total calm.

If the domestic atmosphere becomes so unbearable that your cat's wellbeing is at stake, it may well leave the house (if it is able). But whose fault is that? If the price of their tranquillity is to leave, cats will do it. Take note.

YOUR CAT KNOWS HOW TO ASSERT ITSELF

'I love them, they are so nice and selfish.
Dogs are TOO good and unselfish. They make me feel
uncomfortable. But cats are gloriously human'
L.M. MONTGOMERY, *ANNE OF THE ISLAND*

Many of us find it hard to assert ourselves in front of other people, either out of shyness or lack of confidence. We take a step back, we say little, we behave as if other people are intellectually superior, or at least sufficiently sure of themselves to overpower everyone with their presence, their knowledge, often their idiocies if you actually listen to them.

Who are these 'other people'? They're you and me, for we are all somebody's 'other'. If other people take up more space than you, it's because you let them do so. It's like cupboards: the more you have, the more you fill them.

Do you find that other people invade your space, sometimes even stepping on your toes before walking all over you?

Think of your cat. Try stepping on your cat's paw, just to see their reaction. You'll hear them, and possibly even feel them as they dig their claws into your calf!

Stop getting walked all over. 'Other people' have no right to assert themselves in this way. They have only the space that you grant them; they have only your level of tolerance. They won't stop at crushing your foot. They'll tread you into the dirt, then drown you for good measure!

There is a real difference between having charisma and a strong personality – like your cat – and crushing people in order to impose yourself.

Cats take the space that is their due, without crushing their neighbour, but they do not tolerate any encroachment on that space. They assert themselves quietly. They don't play the tyrant, but neither do they accept a walk-on part.

Know how to assert yourself calmly,
and defend your space at the first attempt
at intrusion. You deserve more than
a walk-on part!

FOOD FOR THOUGHT

'I wish I could write as mysterious as a cat'

EDGAR ALLAN POE

YOUR CAT IS WISE

With their attentive attitude – always listening, like some silent psychologist – a cat resembles a Buddhist teacher or an old sage. But it's maybe more than just an impression. Perhaps we could learn from the way a cat does not exert itself unduly, but sits and contemplates the world.

As the years pass, and we get older, we all acquire a little wisdom and perspective about the world, life and the eternal verities.

How many of us have said at some point: 'I'd like to be twenty again, but knowing everything I know now'? We acquire wisdom with time, whereas cats –

who have no school, no books, no great thinkers, no external frame of reference, not even a large amount of years or experiences – possess a kind of innate wisdom, a wisdom of which we glean just a few snippets, and then only with much reflection, discussion, soul-searching and introspection.

It's a hard road – in more ways than one – to reach a point where we can calmly sit there perusing the horizon with a smile on our face, when a cat has known how to do that practically since birth.

But how can we grasp the ins and outs of this unfathomable, almost mystical, wisdom cats exude?

The truth is that they offer us this wisdom. And if you have a cat, you'll know this. You must have already experienced that moment when, racked with doubts, the same thoughts revolving in your mind, unable to take a step back from it all, you look your cat straight in the eyes and it stares right back at you, as if reading your very soul. And you are filled with a deep conviction that, unlike you, your cat KNOWS. Or at least has KNOWN.

There is something kind in your cat's gaze, evoking that old legend of a Persian emperor who, having gathered his greatest sages, asked them to come up with a phrase that would suit all feelings and situations, good or bad, that a person might encounter in their life. The sages came back to the emperor some time later to deliver the phrase. The message that your cat conveys through its gaze when you are lost, that phrase which has come down through the ages is:

'This too shall pass.'

Yes, for better or for worse, this too shall pass.

We can sometimes spend too much time flailing around, and fall deaf to the essentials of existence. And maybe this is what your cat is telling you with its stillness, its contemplation and benevolent attitude: 'I am here, keeping watch over you and looking out for you. This too shall pass.'

Wisdom is not a subject that can be learned or taught. It is a state, a stance that requires a step back from the agitation of life in order to comprehend it better in its universality. The wise person knows how to sit on the moon in order to gaze at the earth, just like the cat sits on the roof to observe the moon.

YOUR CAT THINKS ABOUT ITSELF FIRST

'A cat does not stroke us, it strokes itself on us'

ANTOINE DE RIVAROL

As we have seen, cats devote most of their lives to ensuring their own wellbeing. And in order to do that, you sometimes have to know how to be a little selfish and think only about yourself.

That doesn't mean being a navel-gazer, narcissist or egocentric, but giving yourself permission to place your personal happiness above that of others at times.

You can't give to others if you don't know how to give to yourself.

Take care of yourself, both physically and psychologically, before anything else; the key to your happiness depends on it.

You'll be able to give and share more, since you'll be happy and fulfilled in your own life.

Don't wait for others before creating your own bubble of wellbeing and tenderness – it depends on you alone. Nobody will do it for you. Moreover, nobody can know what your welfare truly requires.

So take yourself in hand, and, like your cat, construct your territory, your comfort zone and your means of self-fulfilment.

Cultivate little pleasures every day, and never miss an opportunity to give yourself a little gift or an enjoyable moment, because you really do deserve it. Never doubt that!

**Think about yourself and your wellbeing.
Look after yourself. Nobody will do it
better or do more for you than yourself.**

YOUR CAT'S DAY

7.45: BREAKFAST

- Water and milk for your cat, in a clean bowl. Kibble and wet food – from cans or pouches but always good, fresh stuff – served in a clean spot.

- This might seem obvious, but how many of us really take the time to have a proper breakfast? How many of us knock back a quick tea or coffee, leaning against the kitchen sink, not even bothering to prepare a nice slice of toast?

- You've taken care of your cat, now take care of yourself. Having a proper breakfast in a comfortable manner is the best way to start your day, just as it is for your cat.

- Take the time to eat, to make some toast and spread it with that good jam that's been languishing at the back of the fridge. Eat what you like, but take your time and enjoy it.

- Breakfast is the most important meal of the day, as nutritionists are so fond of telling us. It's also a way to look after yourself and your wellbeing, and start the day with a smile.

YOUR CAT ACCEPTS ITSELF AS IT IS, YOUR CAT LOVES ITSELF

'Cats are only human; they have their faults'

KINGSLEY AMIS

It's a fact: we only create pain and disappointment for ourselves when we are unable to accept ourselves as we are. We are all born different, and most of us are dissatisfied with our condition, our body, our social standing. Far too many of us don't love ourselves. We would rather be someone else instead of simply accepting who we are. Accepting ourselves also means discovering the riches and abilities that each of us possesses.

Unlike the cat, we have a tendency to deny what we are, and instead focus on what we would rather be. That's guaranteed to make you miserable.

Does your cat ask itself this? Does your cat wonder what it would be like to be another cat or a different animal? Such a question clearly never enters a cat's mind, because such a question is quite pointless. Cats are proud of what they are, as is proven by their almost haughty attitude to other animals – humans too sometimes.

Your cat has the intelligence not to lumber itself with bogus questions that are liable to promote endless sterile ruminations. Consequently, your cat loves itself for itself, for what it is, and is therefore happy.

Knowing how to accept yourself shouldn't be complicated once you adopt the attitude of your cat, who considers itself to be great just as it is.

We love cats first and foremost because they love themselves. Why not do as they do, without asking too many questions?

Just try this: stand in front of the mirror in the morning and say 'You know I love you?' while laughing.

Seems simple, but try it. You'll have no choice but to smile.

But what does that smile mean? That you love yourself enough or not? From the tone of that smile in the mirror – sad or joyful – you will see the path you must travel to definitively love and accept yourself in your new cat persona.

To be loved, you must start by accepting and loving yourself.

FOOD FOR THOUGHT

'And how do you know that you're mad?'

'To begin with,' said the Cat, 'a dog's not mad.
You grant that?'

'I suppose so,' said Alice.

'Well then,' the Cat went on, 'you see a
dog growls when it's angry, and wags its tail
when it's pleased. Now I growl when I'm pleased,
and wag my tail when I'm angry.

Therefore I'm mad'

LEWIS CARROLL,
ALICE'S ADVENTURES IN WONDERLAND

YOUR CAT HAS A CERTAIN SWAGGER, YOUR CAT IS PROUD

'Dogs believe they are human.
Cats believe they are God'

ANON

We often confuse self-esteem and self-confidence. Although these two notions overlap and complement each other, a person can very well have self-confidence, yet not have much self-esteem, and vice-versa.

Sounds a bit fuzzy? Well, let's say, for example, that you're an excellent salesperson, you have total confidence in your sales abilities and feel confident in yourself when out in the field, and yet each day you tell yourself that your work isn't fulfilling, that it's pointless, that there are better things you could be doing in this world, but that … Lack of self-esteem.

The reverse, just to ram it home: you tell yourself that music is your passion, that you're a talented musician, that you know this because of all the feedback you get from your fans, even though you've found success difficult to achieve because on stage … Lack of self-confidence.

Are you proud of what you are? Of what you do?

The image you have of yourself in what you do, in what you are, is just as important as your self-confidence. If you are in sync with your desires, your needs and your dreams, then self-esteem and self-confidence will often overlap and meld, and you'll attain the peak of your fulfilment and your happiness.

What of the cat, as regards self-esteem and this pride in what they are and what they do? A cat's innate self-esteem and pride in itself is clearly an asset from which we may draw inspiration. Your cat is proud to be a cat, with all the advantages that represents.

Each cat is unique, and they know it. Cats don't have to overdo it to convince themselves or those around them. Your cat is confident, with high self-esteem. Your cat has nothing to prove. To anyone. Your cat simply is.

Simply being a cat is reason enough to swagger with pride.

Be proud of the person you are: in that, you'll be exceptional.

FOOD FOR THOUGHT

'A cat's eyes are windows that
show us another world'

IRISH PROVERB

YOUR CAT IS THE CENTRE OF ATTENTION

'The cat does not offer services. The cat offers itself'
WILLIAM S. BURROUGHS, *THE CAT INSIDE*

Despite their quiet calm, and their 'leave me alone' airs, your cat always seeks to be the centre of attention – as long as they are fond of those humans in their environment. They mince from one lap to another, and will even go so far as to rub themselves against the legs of the only person present who doesn't particularly like cats – as if undertaking a challenge.

Nobody escapes your cat's presence, including the more reticent. Your cat is already the sovereign of your home; and being the centre of attention when you have a few friends round for a drink is a little game of which your cat is very fond.

But how does your cat draw focus? Does it meow for attention? A young cat might, in its first few months, through lack of experience. But any cool and collected cat will merely pad towards you, blinking, hypnotising your guests one by one in just a few seconds, by offering them the 'chance' of stroking its fur, of a little tenderness and attention. Even when you meet a cat for the first time, it will soon become the centre of your focus through its sweetness in calmly approaching, letting itself be touched and even pretending (sometimes) to enjoy it.

Instinctively, we all seek to draw something impalpable from a cat by extending our hand to it. A little calm and serenity. Cats know this, and simply contemplate us. Cats let us do it; they let us soothe ourselves with them. For we all smile when we stroke a cat.

But what has your cat really done to be the centre of attention?

Your cat has given. Given through its way of being, the simple fact of having presented itself to you as a soothing gift you can touch.

A few caresses and suddenly, as if hypnotised, everyone has stopped listening to the conversation. Why? Because the interest your cat has taken in them, the source of life and serenity it has placed within everyone's reach at that moment was worth much more than any philosophical reflections, metaphysical considerations or muddled debate.

To draw attention, be a source, a centre of gravity for your friends and family. Give!

YOUR CAT IS
IMPENETRABLE TO
JUDGEMENT

*'Now a cat, she's got her own opinion about human
beings. She don't say much, but you can tell enough to
make you anxious not to hear the whole of it'*

JEROME K. JEROME

It's an observation that has often amused me: cats
don't care a jot if they're appreciated or not, be it by
people or by other cats.

Cats are independent, solitary characters. On the rare
occasions they attach themselves to humans or to other
animals, it is by choice and with discernment. This means
that quite naturally – and with not a little pleasure – they
ignore what other people think of them, something that
we humans tend to accord far too much importance to.

Cats don't have this need to be loved, appreciated, admired and at the very least accepted by 'other

people'. Cats simply are. Their own view of themselves is all that matters.

Of course we cannot live just by contemplating our own navel, that's not the point. But the balance between self-esteem and what other people think often tilts excessively in the wrong direction.

There is abundant proof all around us of the obsession with appearance in our society. Just look at the media. Personal image has become a cult, not for oneself but for others. Yet it's the biggest fraud we can commit upon ourselves.

Appear cool, appear young, appear rich, appear intelligent, appear tolerant, appear fun, appear open-minded, appear, appear, appear. It's the leitmotif of the last few decades, fuelled by fashion, reality television and social media.

Appear to have talent or appear to be honest, until you manage to convince yourself the lie is real. For all that matters is the current fashion, the latest trend, and acceptance by the majority, so much has the balance shifted in favour of what other people think. How we appear has become more important than what we really are, and therefore what truly makes us happy.

Far too often we submit to this social tyranny of how we should appear, while the cat cares as little for this as it does for its first mouse.

Whether living ferally or in a more or less domesticated group, a cat never adopts the attitude or behaviour of one of its peers. A cat stays true to itself, with its desires, its character and its needs, without the slightest thought of needing to conform to a particular social construct, or present a particular image of itself in order to integrate with the majority – who are themselves often lacking in direction.

Your cat is uncompromising and above all loyal to itself, and you would do well to be inspired by that path. Be as uncompromising as your cat, even if only to reconnect with your desires, even if only to make yourself happier by listening to the still small voice constantly telling you:

Emancipate yourself from other people's views of you. To your own self be true.

YOUR CAT'S DAY

8.15: WASH TIME!

- 🐾 After eating its fill for breakfast, you'll see your cat begin to lick itself at length. It's also shower time for you.

- 🐾 Everyone knows what it's like to take a shower when you're running late. Sometimes the water is barely warm before you step into it. Quick, quick! You're in a rush! Meanwhile your cat slowly runs its tongue the length of one rear paw, then the other. Quite serene.

- 🐾 Beyond the obvious hygiene benefits, a shower is one of those moments in the day when you can and SHOULD take care of yourself. It's also a moment of relaxation, an excellent opportunity to give free rein to your thoughts and let your mind gently wake up to what you have on your schedule.

- 🐾 Women are often better than men in this regard; luxuriating in long periods spent pampering themselves in the bathroom, something men struggle to comprehend. But that is an authentic catlike attitude, and we should all learn from it.

YOUR CAT IS CURIOUS BY NATURE

'There is no more intrepid explorer than a kitten'

JULES CHAMPFLEURY

Cats have an innate curiosity. As soon as they leap from their basket and skitter across the floor, they nose about, sniffing every nook and cranny, examining each object with great concentration and exploring any unknown areas.

Unlike dogs, cats don't throw themselves unthinkingly at every novelty. Your cat progresses cautiously without taking its eyes off the new paper bag or the unexplored hiding place.

Cats have an unbridled curiosity which makes them constantly re-explore their world. Every day is a new discovery, a little scrap of extraordinary fuelled by this boundless curiosity.

We can all benefit from learning a little each day, and being amazed more often.

Some people are more or less observant than others, their minds are more or less focused on always wanting to make new discoveries. Novelty is integral to our wellbeing, it's a kind of oxygen for our minds. We need it like we need air to breathe. Without it, we slowly wither.

For those who don't know how to cultivate this mood-lifting curiosity, simply stick to this basic principle:

Learn something new every day.

The significance, importance or value of this new thing is irrelevant, but learn something each day, even if it's only a single word. You'll remember it for ever.

What matters is to practise this exercise long-term, particularly if you're someone who isn't naturally curious. One moment of curiosity per day means 365 new pieces of knowledge per year, and believe me, it makes all the difference, not only to your ability to perform well in pub quizzes, but above all to your happiness.

Be curious! About everything! You'll live
all the better for it. Amaze yourself.

YOUR CAT IS
IN-DE-PEN-DENT

'Once a cat agrees to live with you, you and the cat
spend the rest of your lives together deciding whether
or not the arrangement is working out'

MICHAEL CUNNINGHAM

Independence is one of your cat's main characteristics.
Cats are not subject to any hierarchy, they don't need
to build any kind of communal life, or live in a tribe,
like other animals.

Your cat's independence is inalienable. Cats live
according to their desires, they don't require the
approval of their kind, and of humans even less.

Why do cats have such an independent existence?

It means they don't have to justify themselves, and
can act purely according to their own wishes, with no
outside pressure, social obligation or accusatory gaze.

This non-negotiable independence is the very foundation of your cat's freedom.

Dependence upon others, be it personal or professional, only subjects us to constraints, which don't always fit with our desires.

Yet, by nature, we cannot be totally independent, as cats are. People have always tended towards living in groups. Despite everything, we all have an interest in regularly measuring the degree of dependence and independence in our lives, in asking ourselves certain questions from time to time:

- How financially independent am I?
- Am I capable of putting up with a few months of celibacy without having a compulsive need to feel loved and desired at each moment, without needing to have one short-term relationship after another to fill the emotional void?
- Do I alone decide the major directions of my life or are they determined by the needs of my partner, parents or children?
- To what extent am I dependent on my work for the money it brings in? Am I so much in debt that I have no other choice than to rack

up overtime, spending weekends and holidays
working?

- Am I so dependent on my partner that I am
capable of accepting everything, enduring
everything, even suffering their humiliations in
silence?
- Do my friends and family have such importance
in my life that I cannot allow myself to contradict
them through my actions and opinions, for fear
that I will offend them and risk losing them?
- Am I obliged to put up with my boss's moods in
order to keep my job, even though there's a better
position waiting for me elsewhere if only I were
to allow myself to apply for it?
- What place do my addictions – be they to
tobacco, alcohol, drugs, food or sport – have in
my life? And consequently, to what extent do
they influence my actions and desires?
- To what extent am I trapped within these
dependencies?
- To what extent do they dictate my life?
- To what extent do I still control my own
existence?

These are all questions we should ask ourselves regularly, starting today, in order to become aware of our level of dependence.

All of us have greater or lesser dependencies in our personal and professional lives – that's a given. What's important is to question these dependencies and assess whether they play major or minor roles in our lives.

In the end, how much weight do I have in my own existence? What are the ingredients of my wellbeing?

We cannot live completely independently, like a cat, but we owe it to ourselves to correct certain tendencies that can evolve, often without us realising.

Work to reconquer a portion of independence in all areas, and you will win your freedom.

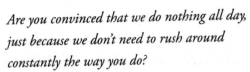

Are you convinced that we do nothing all day, just because we don't need to rush around constantly the way you do?

Contrary to what you think, in reality we are very useful to humans.

When you come home from work, stressed, in an awful mood, full of bad energy that you've accumulated during the day without realising, who do you think frees you of all that?

How is it that after a few moments in our company, stroking us, you feel better, and increasingly soothed, as if by a miracle?

That's what we're there for, us cats. When you touch us, we draw away all those bad vibes that make you so sad, angry, poorly. What's more, you're aware of the soothing effect we have on you, but you think it's merely because of our presence. Yet we do so much more, without you realising.

Each day we treat you for all the ills that life inflicts upon you, because we love you.

ZIGGY

YOUR CAT BRIMS WITH SELF-CONFIDENCE

'There is no such thing as an ordinary cat'

COLETTE

Self-confidence is one of a cat's principal innate strengths, as we saw in that earlier chapter on pride and self-esteem.

Have you ever seen your cat adopt an introverted attitude, as if a little unsure of itself? Of course not. Your cat is proud. Your cat is the best, and knows it. As the old adage goes: 'You're not the best when you think you are, but when you know you are.' It's a small difference, but an important one. And it's the key to self-confidence.

As we have seen, self-confidence depends as much on the acceptance of who you truly are as it does on the pride you feel in what you are – commensurate with your talents or value system.

For example, when your cat approaches you of its own accord, it's thinking, 'I know that you love me', not wondering, 'Do you still love me today?' This certainty is part and parcel of its aura, its charisma, its charm and its beauty. It is one of the reasons why you love your cat.

Far too many people suffer from a lack of self-confidence, while others overflow with it, sometimes for no apparent reason.

As you may have realised, all the chapters in this book overlap with each other, since complete self-confidence depends on an array of abilities – which we have deliberately broken down into separate parts in order to explore them better – but they all commingle and affect each other.

Yes, you must love yourself in order to be confident in yourself. You must be sufficiently independent and uncompromising, and have freed yourself from always wondering 'What will others think?'

Self-confidence is not some airy-fairy concept. It's a set of strengths and abilities that your cat possesses. Learn to incorporate them one by one, and you will live and perform better each day.

People who have confidence in themselves are 'the centre of attention', 'free' and 'charismatic'. They are often quite happy. But they have learned over time how to cultivate all the attributes that have enabled them to develop this self-confidence.

Do as your cat does, and you will be you.

'Have confidence in yourself!' would be a facile phrase for this sort of book. But I can promise you that cultivating the various aspects that form it, as your cat does, will gift you joys and victories in your life, making confidence grow within you naturally.

YOUR CAT KNOWS
HOW TO DELEGATE

'I gave an order to a cat, and he gave it to his tail'

CHINESE PROVERB

Do you tend always to be at your friends' or family's beck and call? Or are you of the opinion that everyone should wait on you and pander to your every whim?

Don't overdo it, but knowing how to be served like a cat can really take the strain out of the everyday.

It's a well-known fact that a cat does nothing, and spends its time being served by others. The cat is king or queen of all it surveys.

You don't have to copy this royal and dominating attitude to the letter, but neither should you be everyone's gopher, always at your family's service. Meeting every expectation, whim and desire of your kids or your partner doesn't make for the most restful existence.

Learn to be served like your cat, and start by delegating the little everyday tasks. You are not your children's slave or skivvy, and it won't do them any harm to take on a few chores – in fact it will help make them more independent. Plus you'll save time, be more efficient, and less tired and stressed. Knowing how to delegate is key. And stop doing tasks yourself just because it's quicker than getting other people to do them.

This also holds true in the workplace. Many company directors and other managers are incapable of trusting others and delegating, so they spend far too much of their time checking and validating their employees' efforts. This creates a culture where employees develop a need to be 'mothered' and will want every minute detail of their work checked and approved. The end result is wasted hours, a loss of autonomy for the employees, and an excess of work for the boss – which may well be you.

Above all, learning to delegate means carving out time for yourself, to do what you like, rather than being a slave to the everyday needs of your family and friends.

And here's another way of seeing things: isn't delegation proof of the trust you have in those closest to you, in your employees, your partner and your children?

Perhaps it would be going too far to say that it's for your own good that your cat expects you to wait on it hand and foot. Remember though:

> Be a cat at work and at home:
> learn to delegate.

FOOD FOR THOUGHT

'The dog may be wonderful prose,
but only the cat is poetry'

FRENCH PROVERB

YOUR CAT'S DAY

8.45: SOFTLY, SOFTLY IN THE MORNING

- Who really knows what a cat does with its day? What we do know is that, in the same way you head off to work in the morning, your cat needs to go out and roam.

- Does your cat rush out of the house at full pelt? No. Your cat shimmies delicately over to the doorway and sticks its nose out to sniff the air – straddling the threshold – which both amuses and annoys you because you can't close the door.

- Why is it that you're in such a hurry when you leave, often having to dash back indoors to pick up your keys or that file you left on the kitchen table? If you were to be a bit more organised, there'd be no need to rush. Look at your cat, strolling tranquilly down the path. Running about like a headless chicken only ends up wasting time and getting you stressed.

- The key to wellbeing is staying calm. Remain cool and collected all day, proceed in a pragmatic, organised manner, and you'll get just as much done, just as quickly, as you would by dashing about in a state of heightened anxiety.

- Follow your cat's lead and start your day with a sure, steady step, and take a few moments to look up to the sky, catch the first rays of sun, and smile.

YOUR CAT KNOWS HOW TO TAKE THE TIME TO LIVE

'Of all animals, the cat alone attains to the contemplative life'

ANDREW LANG

Judging by the way cats simply lie there, or sit, staring at the world, scrutinising the tiniest detail, you might think they're a bunch of lazybones who do nothing all day long. And you wouldn't be wrong … at least when viewed from a human perspective.

There is a marked difference between doing nothing and taking the time to live.

In our current system, doing nothing, being contemplative, breathing, observing, taking the time to live is almost considered suspect. We are told it is imperative to be constantly moving, that we must exploit and fill every minute, accumulate tasks and activities, and never 'waste time'. It has become the norm for our society, a golden rule.

Observing this ceaseless, almost nervous agitation on the part of some of my contemporaries, I cannot help but empathise with cats, who seem to find it amusing to see us pedalling up a sweat on the exercise bike as we answer the phone while watching the TV news … They must think we're insane to exhaust ourselves in this way.

Taking the time to live doesn't mean filling every single moment of our lives, urged on by an ever-present fear of death and the need to have seen and done everything before its inevitable arrival.

On the contrary, taking the time to live means becoming aware of each passing moment, of taking it into consideration, of appropriating it in order to better enjoy it, down to the smallest fraction of a second.

This is what your cat does. For your cat has no notion of time (at least not in the way that we have), nor any notion of eventual death until it occurs – leaving aside the hypothesis that cats do in fact have innate knowledge of there being another side to the mirror, which might also explain their placid attitude in the world of the living, but that's another story.

Taking the time to live means knowing how to fully take advantage of life, and not seeking to accumulate everything you 'should' do/see/visit in a minute-by-minute schedule. For some people, even holidays have become exhausting sprints of sights and activities, until they become more tiring than a week at work.

Sit back, relax, and observe the world around you. Imitate your cat and you'll feel a little serenity return to your life.

There's an adage that goes: 'You took a long time to be born, so take the time to die.' In order to do that, just copy your cat and take the time to live.

YOUR CAT ADAPTS TO
EVERYTHING QUICKLY

'You can throw a cat however you want;
it always falls on its feet'

PROVERB

Ziggy is a cat like any other, except for one thing: he lost his front right paw after being run over by a motorbike when he was less than a year old.

Back then, we lived in the countryside, and he had to defend his territory from other kitties, seduce the local lady cats, satisfy his hunting instincts, and of course clean properly behind his ears.

The latter was easy: after scratching behind his right ear with his left paw, he would come and rub his other ear on me!

But as for the rest, I was quite impressed to see how he behaved the same way on three paws as he had on four in the space of two weeks – once the bandage had been removed, of course.

Not once did he find himself fazed by any obstacle, be it a wall or a fence to climb. Nothing had changed for him, and yet, with one paw less, everything had.

Impressed by his ability to adapt, I observed him for a long time to see how he went about it, and indeed there were a few, barely perceptible, differences. When he ran, he didn't pull himself forward with his front paws like a feline, but propelled himself with his rear paws like a rabbit. And he was incredibly fast!

As for any interlopers who, seeing Ziggy thus amputated, thought they could easily nip into the garden without fear of being chased off: big mistake. Here too, Ziggy adopted a technique all his own: instead of running after the big tom come to flex his muscles, Ziggy took up position in the middle of the garden, quite still, and let the other advance in ever-decreasing circles around him. Once the enemy was close enough, Ziggy stood on his hind legs like a kangaroo, his solitary front paw held high, like that of a boxer. Not comprehending this unusual behaviour, the other cat continued to approach, a little wary but not much. I watched, hypnotised by this calm, this boxer's stance. Once the intruder was within reach, Ziggy let fly with a smashing left hook that stunned the big tom! His single front paw had got seriously muscular with use. Surprised, the intruder beat a retreat, and it was only then that Ziggy chased him off his territory. I was astounded! It was rare that he had to do more than that to see off any cats who attempted to approach the house.

As for the lady cats, it was another matter, since seduction, and the play before coupling, is quite a brutal business with felines. Ziggy had some difficulty in keeping his balance on another cat's back …

Yet the neighbour's puss, who had a crush on Ziggy, quickly understood that if they played the usual games, he wouldn't be able to hold her by the neck like other cats do, and stay on top of her without falling off. So when desire seized her, she positioned herself in front of him, backside in the air, motionless! Ziggy could now comfortably see to both their pleasures.

Cats exceed us in many things, including their ability to adapt, and, in the case of this female, in their understanding.

His handicap never prevented him from living exactly as he did before. There wasn't a ladder or a tree that got the better of him and his missing paw.

We left that house to go and live in the centre of the old town of Lyon. It was a new habitat for Ziggy, with new living conditions. There was no garden, but a narrow street – pretty quiet after 11 p.m. – which had a complex of former workshops with a cat-flap. Ziggy soon adapted to this new location, and devoted many happy nocturnal hours to hunting mice.

We then moved to our current home on a boat – still in Lyon – and there it was simply a case of managing Ziggy's attraction to the passing ducks, lest he fall in the River Saône. Ziggy was initially somewhat overwhelmed at this vast expanse of water stretching before him. But after a few days, he was the new master of the premises, strutting about the cabin roof, surveying his territory from his command post at the highest point, and coming and going along the gangways. Then, wishing to extend his domain, he began descending the steps to stroll along the quayside, have a pee in the grass and keep a close eye on any wayward ducks that came close to the riverbank.

Your cat is an expert at physical adaptation, and adjustment to a new environment. As much as they hate any changes to their lifestyle, they will do their utmost to recreate their cocoon of wellbeing elsewhere, integrating all of the habits which make up their pleasurable existence.

An ability to adapt is a real mark of intelligence.

Where does a cat's capacity for adaptation
come from? Is it because a cat loves life?
Is it because a cat loves its life?
Is it because it loves itself? 'All three',
says Cap'n Ziggy!

FOOD FOR THOUGHT

'If man could be crossed with the cat, it would improve man but deteriorate the cat'

MARK TWAIN

YOUR CAT LOVES CALM

'I believe cats to be spirits come to earth. A cat, I am sure, could walk on a cloud without falling through'

JULES VERNE

'Leave me be! Silence! Calm! Fresh air!' We all dream of saying such things sometimes.

We find ourselves constantly caught up in a whirlwind of noise that wears at our nerves: car horns, slamming train doors, mobile ringtones, and beeping notifications for appointments, text messages and emails.

Your cat loves calm, adores it, seeks it. External calm nourishes their inner calm. Why don't we do the same?

Why not try to take a few moments each day to bathe in absolute calm and silence. Listen only to yourself, your inner voice, your heart beating …

Expand your inner peace in this way, cultivate and nourish it each day to find your exterior calm again. Quite simply: live better.

Do as your cat does, and seek a little calm whenever an opportunity presents itself. And if the environment doesn't lend itself to it, quietly go and find a place to be alone, somewhere only you know. Don't return until you have assuaged your need for calm, and have topped up your energy reserves.

We can put up with all the noise in the world as long as it is not imposed on us, and as long as it doesn't fuel stress and encroach upon our inner calm.

Regularly creating your own calm conditions creates the conditions for your wellbeing, and is the best solution for avoiding ulcers.

YOUR CAT CHOOSES
ITS OWN COMPANY

'A cat will become your friend, if you are worthy of
their affection, but never your slave'

THÉOPHILE GAUTIER

One thing is for sure: cats never burden themselves with relations with other cats, or humans
who don't suit them. They choose their own company,
one by one, loving them all the more.

Why then do we humans spend a considerable
chunk of our lives putting up with insufferable people
who are the antithesis of our values?

Why, out of social convention – and sometimes
cowardice – do we force ourselves to bow and scrape
and smile, expending our time and energy in maintaining – almost under duress – all of these relationships that pollute us?

Choose, as your cat does. It's the simplest option.

Choose who you hang out with, who you love, and who you wish to spend your life with.

The cat who has chosen you will first have tested your affection, your personality and your loyalty. If this cat feels you to be essential to its current and future life, it will love you and remain loyal to you, out of choice.

Life is too short to share it with idiots.

Stop putting up with morons, choose your company, choose your friends.

YOUR CAT'S DAY

12.30: LUNCH BREAK

- Your cat has spent its morning strolling about, so why not do the same?

- Lunch in the gloomy office lounge? Not a great idea. The noisy canteen? Not much better.

- Why not use your lunch break to leave work to eat, preferably outside?

- Take the air, do a spot of window shopping, have a quiet stroll in the park and sit on a bench to eat your lunch. But take the air like the cat does. Wander as your heart desires. Get out, breathe, have a break and, with a nonchalant step, take your fill of the beauty in your environment – all those things you don't usually take the time to look at.

- A good saunter is certainly the best way to escape, breathe and give yourself a chance of making some lovely discoveries, as well as meeting new people ...

- Love at the corner of the street? Yes indeed, but you have to be strolling about to find it ...

YOUR CAT KNOWS HOW TO REST, IT LOVES TO SLEEP

'If stretching were wealth, the cat would be rich'

AFRICAN PROVERB

'Don't wake a sleeping cat' goes the old adage. Look at how much your cat loves to sleep and sleep and sleep. We all love to sleep. So why don't we take every opportunity to do so? Why not choose a little restorative siesta over the supposedly 'urgent' washing up that 'has' to be done, wiped and put away ASAP?

Learn to relax like the cat does. Let yourself slip away to slumberland whenever you have the chance. It's so beneficial, for both mind and body, and you know it. Your cat – lying there softly blinking – has always known this.

Cats, those great artists of vegging out, don't cultivate their sleep, but rather the joy of repeatedly falling asleep …

Sleeping is one of your cat's great pleasures, from light sleeps to deep sleeps where it can be seen running in its dreams. For 'sleeping' means resting, going to sleep and then dreaming. Don't we all have dreams where we'd like to stay awhile? Sometimes we even have dreams we'd like to return to … Shh. It's your inner sanctum.

Taking pleasure in sleeping won't in any way prevent you from 'enjoying life', particularly in the rather inadequate way we tend to understand this phrase.

YOUR CAT KNOWS
WHEN TO SAY NO
(AND READILY DOES SO)

'I will NOT go away. I do NOT wish to go!'

DR SEUSS, *THE CAT IN THE HAT*

Cats hate being told what to do. Obey orders? Not for them!

'If that's what you want, get a dog!' they mutter.

Stubborn to their paw-tips, cats will seldom undertake an action purely because they've been ordered to do so.

Do we humans like obeying orders? Of course not. And yet we put up with them all day long, both at work and at home. And that's not even taking into account the many indirect orders conveyed by those social codes we 'must' follow to the letter.

Learn to say 'no', as a cat does.

Stop endlessly enduring other people's needs, and following directives that don't suit you, or you'll end up living the sort of submissive life where you always say 'yes' when really you would like to say 'no'. Whether it be for a small act of kindness that then turns into a regular custom you find you can no longer stop doing; or taking on tasks that are not part of your job description with such regularity that your colleagues and superiors come to expect it of you, with no offer of financial compensation for the extra workload. Enough!

Learn to say 'no' occasionally to your children, your partner, your boss and your friends, not out of pure selfishness but to preserve your freedom of action and your time. If you always say 'yes' to everyone, how much time will you have left for yourself, to carry out your own tasks or to satisfy your own pleasures?

Learning to say 'no' means knowing how to preserve your time, your capacity for action and your life, as well as winning the respect of your family, friends and colleagues, who sometimes take advantage of this inability to say 'no'.

The balance must be restored between orders and small acts of kindness. None of us should be permanently at the service of anyone else.

'NO means no! Is that clear?'

FOOD FOR THOUGHT

'Cats, as a class, have never completely got over
the snootiness caused by the fact that in Ancient
Egypt they were worshipped as gods'

P.G. WODEHOUSE

YOUR CAT KNOWS HOW TO AVOID CONFLICT (AS MUCH AS POSSIBLE)

'There were only four dissentients, the three dogs and the cat, who was afterwards discovered to have voted on both sides'

GEORGE ORWELL, *ANIMAL FARM*

Cats don't like conflict, except when it comes to defending their territory, 'courting' the neighbour's puss, or giving an intruding tomcat a good hiding.

Have you ever seen a pack of cats gather to battle another pack of cats, on the false pretext of territorial annexation or protection of natural resources? The whole thing orchestrated by two big moggies wearing general's stripes? Never!

The older a cat gets, the more it employs stratagems to get its enemy to flee, so avoiding conflict.

Ziggy has an unbeatable trick he uses when a large tomcat enters his territory at night. As soon as he senses danger approaching, he hides and waits. The first time I heard him growling, low and loud, it was quite terrifying. Upon entering the garden, I spied another cat dashing away as fast as it could. Ziggy was nowhere to be seen. I called him, but he didn't come.

It was only when I went back inside that I realised his technique: he was hiding behind a few branches of Virginia creeper in the shadow of the outside window ledge, boosting his voice (honestly, he sounded like a tiger), which served to warn the intruder of his apparent physical size without him having to show himself. If the other cat remained in the vicinity, he would know what to expect in the coming fight. Nine times out of ten it worked. The cat fled, and Ziggy remained at his hidden sentry post until he was sure that the other had crossed back over the border of his territory. Then he came out and continued his patrol. Despite his three paws, Ziggy's nighttime weapons for avoiding conflict were cunning, strategy and make-believe.

Cats are not bellicose scrappers. They are proud, and will always avoid having to fight, as long as their territory is not under threat. It's a precept that I read in Sun Tzu's *The Art of War*. Perhaps Sun Tzu, writing over two and a half thousand years ago, was also inspired by a cat? *The Art of War* has become a key text for strategists and military leaders, although some of them have clearly forgotten its teachings …

Cats have an interesting way of managing conflicts, compared with the sparring that humans still like to indulge in – a practice as old as it is useless.

In a conflict, there are always two losers. Cats have long known this.

Insofar as possible: avoid conflicts.

YOUR CAT ADORES ITS HOME, AND MARKS OUT ITS TERRITORY

'Happy is the home with at least one cat'

ITALIAN PROVERB

Cats adore their home, whatever the size. Their home is their domain, and they are the sole masters of the place. People who have a cat will often say, with a smile: 'The cat doesn't live with me. I live with the cat!'

With a cat's propensity to be the boss, to 'delegate', to get others to serve them, to be stubborn and do only that which pleases them, some cat owners let themselves – out of love – become overwhelmed by their cat's needs and desires. Everyone needs to set their boundaries in order to live in harmony.

But what interests us here is the love, attention and protection that a cat accords to its house, its territory.

It is worth noting that a cat living in the countryside may have a territory covering eight to ten acres – even if they are domesticated. So don't be surprised by your cat's very long walks, since it spends much of its time keeping watch over its domain.

That said, cats are extremely attached to their home, even if it's just a one-bedroom flat, for it represents the very heart of their world of comfort, and the locus of their physical and psychological wellbeing.

Have you ever paid attention to the interior of your friends' homes, their cleanliness, tidiness and decoration? Do they spend much time there? Or are they out most of the time? Are you often invited round?

If you look closely, can't you see a link between these people's homes and their emotional state? There is very often a connection between a person's internal happiness and the upkeep and decoration of their living space. It's like a mirror effect, a direct visualisation of their state of mind, even the image they have of themselves.

What about you? How do you feel at home? What are the walls and furniture like? Do you find it to be a comfortable and relaxing place? Do you enjoy having friends round for dinner? Are you proud to show off your home? Have you got a comfy sofa, covered in cushions and throws, for those Sundays snuggled up with a film and a bottle of wine? Have you created all of the conditions for your own wellbeing?

Unlike your cat, you don't need to mark your territory (!). Your home should also be a sanctuary, somewhere for you to truly relax, recharge your batteries and cut yourself off from the hustle and bustle outside, just for a while.

Your home is the nerve centre of your happiness, and you can constantly expand its frontiers – as your cat does – in concentric circles. There's your immediate neighbourhood, the local shops and businesses you get to know, the little park at the corner of the street where you go to read quietly in summer. Like your cat, you can extend your territory, your comfort zone, your safety perimeter.

Your cocoon should be a cosy nest you can always return to whenever you need to relax, take care of yourself, re-centre, and receive the people you love.

Home sweet home! Cultivate the comfort and aesthetics of your little gilded palace, and you'll feel so much better.

1.15: OBLIGATORY SIESTA

❀ Although your cat will surely spend half the afternoon sleeping, you usually won't be able to do the same.

❀ However, following lunch and a relaxing stroll, you will surely still have a quarter of an hour, maybe even thirty minutes, left before returning to your desk.

❀ Why not try a fifteen-minute micro-siesta? You will feel re-energised as if you had slept for several hours.

❀ More and more companies are introducing this practice in order to make their staff more efficient. The cat's siesta has become a business tool!

❀ Above all, it's a means of recovering from a lack of sleep, to boost your energy or in anticipation of a big night out with your friends.

YOUR CAT TRUSTS YOU

*'It is no compliment to be the stupidly idolised master
of a dog whose instinct it is to idolise, but it is a
very distinct tribute to be chosen as the friend and
confidant of a philosophic cat'*

H.P. LOVECRAFT, 'CATS AND DOGS'

Once a cat has chosen you as a life companion, they will trust you fully, absolutely, almost blindly. For example, when you stroke your cat, it may roll over on its back, a position that cats will never naturally put themselves in (except when they are somewhere they feel entirely safe), because it is much too vulnerable a position and they would find it too difficult to flee or defend themselves. And yet, caress by caress, and after many kisses and other gestures of affection, you will win your cat's trust and it will sit on your lap or alongside you, in the most improbable positions, to be stroked again and again, to play and to have its belly scratched.

This deep trust can be displayed in various ways, but certain behaviours are clear indicators of it.

How much do we trust other people?

It often happens that we find it hard to trust again, following disappointment in love or friendship. As much as we believe the other person, we always remain vigilant, attentive to the slightest sign of something we interpret (often wrongly) as a false step to come, or a little lie in waiting.

Such a suspicious attitude can do us a real disservice in our lives. How can you be happy if you're constantly living in fear of being betrayed by someone else at any moment? It's impossible.

There is no other way of finding tranquillity and zest for love again than by relearning to trust, blindly, almost as cats do.

But, like your cat, you shouldn't place your trust in just anyone, nor immediately open wide the door to your feelings and to your life.

Follow your instinct with the people you meet; it will never let you down. And as soon as you feel you have met the right person, be it in friendship or in love, don't shut yourself off from happiness by remaining in a stance of fear and distrust.

Open the sluice gates of your heart, let yourself go, and trust. There won't be any other choice or possible path to take, if you want to live this chance at happiness to the full.

**Tame your fears. Love and trust
with discernment.**

YOUR CAT IS A
NATURAL BOSS

'When the cat's away, the mice will play'

PROVERB

C ats are excellent managers, perfect bosses, for they keep an eye on things without really doing anything. They don't need to yell: a look is enough to garner respect. A cat simply is, and its presence alone is sufficient to intimidate the mice.

While I was writing this book, Ziggy lay stretched out on my pile of papers, keeping a close eye on me to ensure I remained focused on the task at hand and didn't daydream. It was no doubt largely thanks to him that the manuscript was delivered on time.

As we have already seen, being a cat at work means knowing how to delegate, that's the main thing. Be it for the proper organisation of the tasks and the firm, or for your colleagues' validation and autonomy. But it also means knowing how to be present, to keep an eye on things, see without being seen, and set an example.

Whether or not you are the boss, a catlike attitude is very well suited to a professional context. Take these examples:

- Don't expend your energies unnecessarily. Ration your work and the time allocated to complete it, according to the task's importance. (Cat says: 'Who cares about that spider? I'm not moving until a mouse comes along.')
- Don't bustle about just to give the impression of being snowed under. It only creates useless stress for your colleagues. (Cat says: 'Stop flailing about with your vacuum cleaner, you're making my head spin!')
- Be efficient when necessary. Deal with problems immediately. (Cat says: 'What do you think you're doing, you lumbering fool? Don't move, I'll sort you out!')
- Always be watchful without being noticed, in order to stay abreast of the latest news about what's happening in the company. (Cat says: 'I

know it's you who's tickling me with a feather.
Come a little closer, then you will know!')

- Be responsive if required. Know how to make
  that special effort. (Cat says: 'A mole invasion in
  the garden? Fine, I'll work a double-shift! We'll
  soon get them shifted!')

- Regularly take a coffee break with colleagues
  to catch up on the office gossip and maintain
  your social relations. (Cat says: 'The kibble
  distributor is still full, right? So let's break open
  the sardines!')

- Don't pretend to work. Someone will always
  notice. (Cat: 'I've visited all the checkpoints on
  the territory. Security's fine. Let me sleep now!')

- Don't pretend to be overwhelmed, it's often a
  sign of inefficiency. (Cat: 'Worry not, it's all
  under control. Rrrr …')

**And if you're the boss, be like your cat:
always maintain a firm yet benevolent
attitude, encourage with a glance,
and be present.**

Boss or not, when you're at work, always give the best of yourself without talking a lot of hot air.

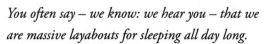

You often say — we know: we hear you — that we are massive layabouts for sleeping all day long.

Firstly, you should know that even if we sleep in the early evening for a few hours, we prefer to live by night, unlike you lot. You don't realise this, because you're asleep.

Secondly, if we sleep so much during the day, it's because of you, for these sleep sessions allow us to get rid of all the bad vibes and thoughts we've relieved you of. We can't hang on to them. We too must cleanse our mind and our soul, and that's what our sleep is for.

Know too that we can also relieve the bad moods of several members of your family, for we can soothe you one by one, but our restorative sleep will only be the longer for it.

If you've had the good sense to take in a couple of cats from when they were born, they can share this task within your family. However, don't lumber us with a kitten once we're already well settled, or there'll be a ruckus all over the house, believe you me!

ZIGGY

YOUR CAT IS TENACIOUS

'Never try to outstubborn a cat'

ROBERT A. HEINLEIN

Stubborn, yes, tenacious even more so. You can call for your cat as often as you like while it is lying on the grass, it won't stir, not even turn its head. Your cat is capable of staking out a mouse-hole for hours on end, waiting for the rodent to emerge. Patience, tenacity: you can watch your cat do this for a good chunk of the day without it getting bored or giving up. It's a real life lesson.

It's about perseverance – worthy of respect – until the objective of catching that mouse is attained. Your cat won't count the passing hours or the accumulated fatigue, whereas we all too often give up when we're in sight of our goal. Your cat's attitude is worth some consideration.

The patience your cat employs to obtain what it desires is equalled only by its tenacity. We can only admire it and strive to act similarly.

'Never give up!' is your cat's credo, and it will stick to it, come what may.

Be patient and tenacious in everything you undertake. Never give up!

YOUR CAT IS ALWAYS CAUTIOUS

'The cat loves fish, but hates wet feet'

MEDIEVAL PROVERB

Cats are not hotheads, and they always learn from their misadventures. Your cat will never approach a new place, a car or an object without first observing it for a long time and taking infinite precautions. Cats avoid putting themselves in unnecessary danger. Anything new is first inspected, sniffed and analysed in minute detail.

Being cautious often avoids problems, conflicts and accidents. But – no doubt from lack of instinct – humans have always accumulated their knowledge and experience through seizing the smouldering ember with both hands in order to understand that it burns. It's a weird way of going about things, when you think about it. Humans don't know anything unless they have learned it. Can you imagine your cat walking over glowing ashes?

How many of us have fallen sick after eating spoiled food without realising it? And yet, how many times have you seen your cat turn up its nose and not touch the food bowl if the contents have dried out a bit, or refuse to eat the piece of ham you offer until it has sniffed it from every angle?

There is little chance of your cat poisoning itself, for your cat uses its senses and is cautious, including about what it eats.

Humans are often intrepid by nature, and therefore imprudent, just like a child who must be warned about everything, taught everything and protected from any danger. But who taught your cat that fire burns, that water drowns and that big, barking dogs should be given a wide berth? Who taught your cat that those large, noisy things rolling down the street are cars that can run you over? Cats know these things by instinct, they sense danger, unlike a child.

We have lost many of our instincts, many of our senses, even in our relations with people. How many of us have at some point said: 'I just knew he was going to do that to me. I've had a funny feeling about him from the start.'

Your instinct was right. The truth about this person formed your perception of them, and yet, did you follow your instinct when this feeling of rejection of the other first came upon you? No. We often prefer reason to instinct. It's such a pity when, as time goes by, we realise that our instinct never fails us, and that it always guides us, for the good of our wellbeing, towards caution.

First impressions never lie. For a little more caution in the future, try to reconnect with your most primal instincts, listen to yourself and trust yourself. You will never regret it.

When there is a doubt, there is no doubt. Follow your instinct!

YOUR CAT'S DAY

6.30: HOME SWEET HOME, RETURN TO THE FOLD

🐾 A moment of relaxation, hugs, caresses. The laundry and the voicemails can wait. Be like your cat and unwind after your working day. There's no point scrambling to do the outstanding household chores. Slip into something more comfortable and take half an hour to sit down in peace, maybe putting some music on.

🐾 Breathe a while before joyfully starting the second part of your day, the part that's all about you, your whims and desires, perhaps phone a few friends ...

🐾 At this time of day, your cat's only concern is most probably: 'Shouldn't my dinner be ready soon?' It's a moment of great personal pleasure, since your cat knows that you will shortly take the time – unlike this morning – to open a pouch of salmon in jelly, the sort your cat loves so much.

🐾 Six thirty in the evening is a little moment of relaxation, both for your cat and for you, a point where the day shifts from activity to relaxation. The best thing is not to carry your day's fatigue or stress into your little world of comfort for the evening.

YOUR CAT HAS A HUGE NEED FOR LOVE

'Cats are beings made to accumulate caresses'

STÉPHANE MALLARMÉ

We all need hugs, kisses, caresses and other gestures of affection. And though many of us sometimes find ourselves with a deficiency of love, cats never hesitate to come and demand some tenderness from you when they require it.

Your cat sometimes needs to feel this emotional closeness with you, in the same way that we sometimes need to bury ourselves in a deep embrace with our partner and hold them tight.

Freud describes the first trauma in our life as being when the umbilical cord, that physical link to our mother and to her love, is severed at birth. Forever after, we try to re-establish that emotional link through all our relationships with others, be it love or friendship.

The more we suffer a lack of affection, the more we will seek it from others, drawing on it until we're full, overflowing. Just like the cat, we withdraw physically from this source once we're satiated with love … before returning to it again.

The frequency of our need for love also depends upon the love we have for ourselves. Some people are very cuddly, others not so much, for we don't all require the same 'dose' each day. But all of us need tenderness, hugs and emotional warmth to a certain extent.

We draw it from our partner and also from our cat, just like the cat draws it from us – think of all those times when your cat buries its head lovingly under your arm. That's its way of drawing some love from you. See how it practically drools with need for this tenderness. It's quite different from an everyday cuddle of simple wellbeing. And once that need for love and affection is assuaged, your cat will slip off your lap and go about its business.

We are just the same: needing, expecting, waiting for this vital love that each of us requires.

Just like the cat, or like a flower, we wilt a little more each day when deprived of love. It is for that reason that the human heart has never been able to do without this driving force called love.

> We all need love. But you need to know
> how to give it in order to receive it.
> It's a key condition for our happiness.
> What would life be like without love?

YOUR CAT IS SERENE
BY NATURE

'The smallest feline is a masterpiece'

LEONARDO DA VINCI

M oving, constantly moving, bustling about is what many of us do, as if we were incapable of staying still for a single moment, so caught up are we in the incessant rhythm of big-city living, with the tons of stress it pours over us and which we carry home.

You've barely got back from work, you chuck your coat onto the sofa and you flit from dirty laundry to outstanding bills, a broom in one hand and a duster in the other.

Your cat watches you rushing between the kitchen, the lounge and the study. You wonder why it is looking at you so strangely. Yes, it's clear that you're disturbing your cat, but also that it is trying to figure out whether you've had a sudden attack of serious idiocy.

Pick up the remote control for your DVD player and press 'Pause'. This is not just a figure of speech; do it for real. Take a long breath in, then breathe out slowly. You will feel a deep, inner peace, as if you had just placed your baggage on the ground. A smile will light up your face, and, through this action and your cat's gaze – which hasn't left you for a second – you will become aware of having switched from the frenzy of a working day into the useless frenzy of another sort of working day, made of hyperactivity and nerves.

Of course household chores need to be done, but there is no reason not to approach them in a calmer, stress-free manner.

If, however, you continue bustling about, you will see your cat calmly stand up and pad away to find a calmer place to settle down and clean itself, and maybe doze. You might even fancy you see your cat shake its head while saying to itself: 'Incorrigible human! Hardly home, and already it's stress-central here. I'm off to hunker down in that pile of clean sweaters in the bedroom. Should be nice and tranquil there for a little while, at least.'

And, throwing a final meow in your direction before steering a path for those soft, sweet-smelling clothes that you'll only have to clean again later, you might comprehend something like: 'Hey, while you're at it, don't forget to fill my bowl with kibble and change my litter, it fair stinks in there!'

Stop bustling about all over the place: it's such a waste of energy. Learn to be serene.

FOOD FOR THOUGHT

'Cats are mysterious folk. There is more passing
in their minds than we are aware of'

SIR WALTER SCOTT

YOUR CAT KNOWS WHAT IT WANTS, AND IS DIRECT ABOUT IT

'There are many intelligent beings in the universe.
Most of them are owned by cats'

OLD POLISH PROVERB

Cats don't beat about the bush when they want something from you; they will pester you until they get what they want. Cats are demanding, and you can't dupe them with a new brand of kibble if they're not crazy about it. At best, your cat will sulk, or knock over the bowl, and you'll be forced to put the new pack away in the cupboard and go out and buy the usual brand. Your cat knows what it wants and will stick to its guns.

By the same token, you will never be able to force your cat to come in at night if it's strolling about or happily ensconced in a flowerbed two feet away from you.

Cats are excellent hunters, and when they are pursuing their prey nothing can distract them from their objective. This stubborn obstinacy is the cat's great quality. Cats always know what they want. There's no point even trying to negotiate.

How often should we ourselves have to make compromises according to some external factor?

There's a saying that goes: 'I don't really know what I want, but at least I know what I don't want.' I only half-like this saying, which often serves to cover up true desires which we sweep under the carpet, not believing ourselves capable of attaining them.

'What do you really want?' is a question that we should all ask ourselves regularly and with the utmost honesty. All too often we end up settling for what our friends and family 'want' or 'expect' of us, rather than what we 'believe' we are made for. We forget the motivations and desires that truly drive us.

'What do you really want?' Cats know exactly what they want, and spend their whole life focused on that alone.

Knowing what you want is one thing. The second step is to give yourself the means to achieve it, to be demanding and direct in your aspirations. Don't beat about the bush.

This mania we all have, to a greater or lesser extent, of avoiding saying exactly what we wish to say or clearly asking for what we want, is exhausting in more ways than one.

Be straightforward. Don't be scared to call a spade a spade, to tackle subjects directly, to tell the truth as it appears, and to state explicitly what you desire. Be direct, and you'll save both time and energy.

Finally, although cats know what they want, they do more than merely demand it through their attitude or behaviour (at least we humans are fortunate to have the power of speech): they act.

Be direct, ask. 'I want, I can, I do!' should become as natural for you as proud whiskers are for a cat.

YOUR CAT DARES TO ASK (ALL THE TIME)

As we have seen in the previous chapter, once we have clearly identified, formulated and expressed our desires, we sometimes require a lever, a trigger, a little help.

Often we don't dare ask for help with our work, or if we have issues in our personal life. Why not? Shame, perhaps. The fear of seeing this help refused. Some reticence in showing our true colours. Or a feeling of begging. And the shame is even stronger when there are serious money problems. We don't ask for help out of vanity and also misplaced pride.

But your cat does ask for things. It will be demanding when it is hungry, wants to go out for a walk or feels like a cuddle. Even when you're sleeping, your cat will shamelessly come and wake you up to ensure you attend to whatever it wants at that moment.

We too have everything to gain from asking for help around us when we need it. And the most surprising thing is that there is always someone who will be delighted to help you … as long as you ask them.

How often have you heard: 'But you should have asked! Why didn't you mention this to me then? I could have helped you.'

Sometimes the simplest solution is just to ask.

Your cat is always right. It dares to ask.

Dare to ask for help. Some people will be delighted to give you a hand, because they will feel that you value them.

YOUR CAT'S DAY

7.30: DINNERTIME

- If lunch was a bit rushed, owing to your short break, evening is an opportunity to treat yourself and cook a nice meal.

- Your cat has persuaded you to serve its favourite finely-chopped salmon in jelly, so there is no reason why you should content yourself with a tin of ravioli half-warmed up in the microwave and sprinkled with some grated cheddar you found at the back of the fridge.

- Cooking with or for someone else is always easier of course, but if you're on your own, try to find some simple recipes you can enjoy solo.

- And do bother to get a decent plate out, even if it's just to eat a Chinese takeaway – much nicer than picking noodles out of a greasy box. Nurture your wellbeing down to the smallest detail. And if you're living with someone, take advantage of this moment to sip a glass of wine, discuss your day or gently rib them about under-seasoning the dish or cutting the potatoes wrong. A little banter goes a long way to take the drudgery out of cooking at the end of a working day, as well as making for a very pleasurable evening.

YOUR CAT IS
ALWAYS HONEST

We all tell fibs, sometimes. And the first person we lie to is ourselves. But those little accommodations with the truth never bring us much pleasure. On the contrary, we're embarrassed by them, and not very proud of ourselves.

Cats never hide their qualms, their feelings and desires. They are always transparent and consistent in their attitude and with what is in their minds.

'Why do otherwise?' they might wonder. Observing them, one might agree. After all, why act any other way than honestly towards others and towards oneself? At the end of the day, it's the simplest approach.

If you're honest, there are no games to play, no stance to adopt, no lies to remember so that you don't contradict yourself. You don't have to maintain a certain line, keep a particular attitude or undertake tasks stemming from something you boasted of in order to remain consistent vis-à-vis those around you, and not be taken for a massive mythomaniac.

Lying is exhausting. Particularly if you want to keep it up. Indeed, all compulsive liars end up being found out sooner or later, for the more they lie, the harder it is to maintain the accumulating falsehoods, which grow in complexity and start feeding into each other.

But you can stop with the fibs and the mythomania by being lazy and simply telling the truth. Be honest and transparent like the cat, and, as we have seen, you will gain in charisma and credibility.

Be honest for the sake of the trust that others will place in you, for your image, your peace of mind and your self-esteem.

**Be honest, you have everything
to gain from it.**

YOUR CAT IS SILENT AND OBSERVANT

'I am as vigilant as a cat to steal cream'
WILLIAM SHAKESPEARE, *HENRY IV, PART I*

Feral cats don't meow, except during periods of reproduction, when they produce something more akin to a roar to keep their rivals at bay.

When a cat is just a kitten, it will meow to assert itself, to be heard, but as the months pass, it will become increasingly quieter.

The higher-pitched meow of an adult cat is aimed solely at us humans. It is an attempt to speak to us, and of course we can't understand a thing. So most of the time, cats stop the meowing and turn back to their thoughts, their observations and their wellbeing. There are no sterile discussions with another cat or with a human who can't understand anything.

Just like the kitten, we babble away constantly when we're children in order to express ourselves. But as we get older and our language skills advance, we talk more and more, even if it's sometimes a whole load of nonsense.

Unlike us, cats become 'old adults' very quickly, and therefore learn to keep their counsel much faster. They watch in silence, not missing a single thing we do, or any changes to their environment, but it is rare that they will comment on anything.

Our propensity to express ourselves about everything all of the time (and being a big chatterbox myself, I am more than familiar with what I'm talking about) sometimes obscures an important element for our wellbeing: learning to keep quiet.

And as a big chatterbox I know all too well that sometimes we really do talk a lot of rubbish. There are times when we even go too far, or are in a bad mood, and what we say is misconstrued. It wasn't what we meant to say, but it's too late and the words are out there, unfiltered.

Learning to keep your counsel means controlling your impulsiveness, avoiding talking drivel, and reflecting on and weighing up your thoughts before expressing them. It also means listening to what others have to say, not monopolising a conversation, and not asserting your own opinion as the last word on the matter.

Learning to keep your counsel means keeping a slight distance, and maintaining a little secrecy in your life. Be sincere, but don't be absolutely transparent about everything with everyone all of the time, so as to protect yourself from the worst of the backbiters.

Expressing yourself is not the same as laying it on thick, and while discussion is vital, observation and listening are sometimes just as persuasive as any argument.

Learn to keep your counsel. Learn to no longer be the centre of everything at every moment through talking. Listen in order to learn, and know when to keep quiet so as to have more impact when you do speak.

FOOD FOR THOUGHT

'If a fish is the movement of water embodied,
given shape, then a cat is a diagram and
pattern of subtle air'

DORIS LESSING

YOUR CAT IS A
SINCERE FRIEND

'Ne'er shall thy now expiring puss forget
To thy kind care her long-enduring debt,
Nor shall the joys that painless realms decree
Efface the comforts once bestowed by thee'

ANNA SEWARD,

'AN OLD CAT'S DYING SOLILOQUY'

If your cat accepts you into its world, it will become your faithful, steadfast friend. Consequently, your cat will take care of you each day. It will pad up to you, meowing gently, to see how you're doing, will listen to your complaining and will know how to reassure and console you. Your cat will be there for you at every moment.

But are we humans just as present, just as attentive to our own friends? Honestly, don't we occasionally let some relationships slide a bit, even though they have taken so long to develop?

We should follow the example of our cats, and take the loyalty, abnegation, tenderness and friendship they show us and apply it to our friends almost to the letter.

Life's vicissitudes and changes mean that we often take voluntary or involuntary breaks from our nearest and dearest.

The case of the new romantic relationship is one that we are all familiar with. Caught up in the passion of our newly forming couple, we forget the world around us for a few weeks, even a few months. It's quite understandable, and things go back to normal after a while – once the heady days of flourishing romance are behind us – and we reinforce those relations we'd forgotten for a bit.

But it also happens that we decide – consciously or not – to change our life completely, and we don't return to those who were always there for us year after year. We devote ourselves to our new love instead. It's a form of brazen selfishness that can make our friends feel abandoned, even betrayed.

'I no longer see her any more, ever since she got together with X.' We have all heard or said that phrase, with disappointment, at one time in our life or another.

We could learn a lot from cats about loyalty in friendship. For a cat is simply there, from the first day to the last, with neither games nor calculations.

Cats can be capable of more humanity than us humans, whereas we are sometimes tempted to turn inward and focus on our little lives, forgetting all that has been given and all that has been said.

A friendship can be as powerful as a romantic relationship, if not more so, in that it often lasts much longer …

Sacrificing friendship for the rush of love, on the pretext of adhering to society's codes that dictate we should all 'settle down' once we reach a certain age, is already in itself a kind of calculation, an attempt to appear to be 'doing the proper thing'. It's also the best way of ensuring that, if a break-up occurs, your friends will no longer be there to support you.

Maintain your friendships. They are one of the most precious treasures in your life. Never sacrifice them.

YOUR CAT FOCUSES ON THE ESSENTIAL

*'What I like about the cat is the indifference
with which it moves between luxurious
surroundings and its native gutter'*

CHATEAUBRIAND

I was observing how my cat Ziggy is so attentive to his personal hygiene and his appearance, yet will happily root about in the filthiest dumpster, when the surprising realisation came to me that not only does he care not a jot for luxury and material things, but in fact he couldn't give two hoots about his appearance either.

I also recall a friend's magnificent white angora cat with green eyes who regularly returned from its walks as dirty as could be after rolling around in cellars, and would settle down on the sofa cushions to give itself a thorough clean. The cat loved both environments and really didn't care about looking like a dirty dish-cloth as it strolled down the street, returning from its escapades.

We could all learn how to detach ourselves from our environment and from material things, just for a bit, and try not to give too much importance to them, as well as spending a lot less time looking at ourselves in the mirror getting our appearance just right. It would help us to find a little humility, and a little truth.

Cats cultivate neither materialism nor social status; their pleasures and desires are all that count. What do others think? What about their opinions and judgement? Cats don't give a damn, as we have already seen.

What does a cat think when it wants something, or is poised to make a fresh discovery? 'Yeah, I'm going to get real dirty, so what? I'll clean myself after. Now, where did that big thing with a long tail go? Ah, that way! Under that pile of filthy crap! Let's go!'

Indulge in what you like when you want to, without worrying about the rest too much.

Don't give too much importance to material things, for you know what they say: 'The things you own end up owning you.'

YOUR CAT'S DAY

8.30: A RELAXING EVENING

- Cushions, sofa, a delight for any cat looking to relax after a hard day.

- 'What are they still doing at their desk, bashing away frenetically at the keyboard?' your cat surely wonders, before leaping up and walking over the keys, tickling your nose with its tail. And you grumble because you have to 'get this thing finished'.

- Your cat serves to remind you that there is a time for everything, for work, for family, for your partner, for relaxation, and for your cat of course.

- It's 8.30 p.m. and your cat feels that it is no longer time to 'get this thing finished', but to 'shut up shop'.

- I didn't listen to Ziggy most of the time when he stretched out on the desk beside me after umpteen comings and goings between my lap and the keyboard, rubbing his nose on the corner of the screen. It was 10 or 11 p.m. and I was getting bogged down in my writing without really making much progress.

- Who was right at that moment in time? A relaxing evening lost for little actual work.

- I now impose a rule upon myself: 9 p.m. at the latest, I step away from my desk. Have a pleasant evening!

YOUR CAT ALWAYS REMAINS NATURAL

'A cat may go to a monastery, but she remains a cat'
ETHIOPIAN PROVERB

No false seduction, role-play or borrowed style: your cat never puts on a costume or assumes a particular attitude when approaching you. Whatever it desires or requests, your cat will always do it in line with its personality.

Your cat is honest, as we have seen, because it's much simpler that way. So why would your cat put on an act in order to be taken for something it is not? What good would it do them?

And what good does it do us when we do it – often out of lack of confidence? Nothing. We are lying to ourselves again, and we are lying to others. And the worst is that we are convinced that this disguise we've just put on, to deal with a particular situation or certain individuals, will be more credible than what we are deep down inside. What stupidity!

How can a cardboard-cutout film set replace the majesty of a real mountain or a raging ocean?

When we lie – out of fear of not measuring up – we make ourselves vulnerable to being seen through, devoid of either charm or charisma.

There is nothing plasticky about our natural state. It radiates everything that we are. It makes us beautiful, attractive and credible in other people's eyes.

Being natural is the pledge of what we are, with no sham or subterfuge. Knowing how to remain natural in every situation and accepting who we are remains the best way not only to be appreciated but to really impress people. Never underestimate yourself.

Remain natural in all circumstances.

YOUR CAT IS HUMBLE
AND INDULGENT

*'A cat is not bound to live by the
laws of a lion's nature'*

SPINOZA

We all have a tendency to sometimes set the bar
a little high, to be hard on ourselves and even
beat ourselves up about things.

Be ambitious, sure; give the best of yourself, of
course; but it's equally important to know how to be
kind to yourself in the event of a setback.

It's important to be honest and to give your utmost
to any job or project, but nobody can expect you to
excel at everything, all of the time, to the point of
making yourself ill.

What does this all have to do with what you can
learn from your cat? It's all summed up in the quote

129

from Spinoza on the previous page. Your cat may be a feline, like the lion, but your cat doesn't exhaust itself all day long trying to be as strong and as fast as a lion. Your cat is not and never will be the king of the jungle. Perhaps it isn't even the boss among the other cats in the neighbourhood. But so what? Does that prevent your cat from living its life to the full and being happy? Does it spend its time wanting to attain a position or acquire a status it knows it will never reach? Does it hold itself to blame for things it cannot control?

Neither a little humility nor a little acceptance of yourself will prevent you from being proud of what you are and what you do. Should you stop singing just because you're not Freddie Mercury? Should you stop painting just because you're not Paul Cézanne? Does a lack of those talents make you a less valuable human being? Or just different?

Do the best with what you are and continue to progress, for even if your cat knows it will never be a lion, that won't prevent it leaping, running, hunting and being the king of your sofa even if it can't be the king of the jungle.

Be humble in what you do. Be kind to yourself. But whatever you do – Do!

Some of you like sleeping with us, but often, at bedtime, we find ourselves on the other side of the bedroom door. It's true that when we're young, we move around a bit, and since we don't sleep a lot at night, we feel like playing in the bed. But, you know, we calm down after a few years, so open the door to us and we'll doze peacefully at your feet.

For if we come to your bed, it's not just for the warm cushions and quilt, it's also to protect you.

Who else keeps watch at night to stop evil spirits entering your home and disturbing you while you sleep?

This is also our mission. We sleep with you so we can protect you better. Believe me or not, but even if you reckon that's all a bit too mystical, just think about it.

ZIGGY

YOUR CAT KNOWS HOW TO SEE THE FUN IN EVERYTHING

*'When I play with my cat, who knows whether it has
more fun with me than I do with it?'*

MICHEL DE MONTAIGNE

We sometimes wonder if life is serious when we learn the hard way. So it's important to know how to have fun, in order to mitigate its sometimes darker aspects or simply to choose to approach a situation from another angle (glass half full or half empty?).

Knowing how to have fun is a key condition for happiness. Overly serious people, forever stuck in their fanciful thoughts, sometimes end up incapable of knowing how to play, have fun and laugh; they are virtually incapable of smiling.

Play is one of your cat's main occupations, and hunting is a part of that, as cruel as this can seem when you see it tossing a maimed field mouse about for hours, letting the poor thing escape for a few inches before pouncing on it again. But it's your cat's way of amusing itself, just as we humans have invented myriad ways of laughing and having fun.

Know how to laugh (and above all how to laugh about everything), know how to not take yourself too seriously, know how to put your social standing to one side – just think of those times when you hear people say something like: 'I'm sure you understand that I couldn't allow myself to do that, it would undermine my position.'

Self-image, cultivated pretences … We must forget everything, all of those human traits that prevent us from having fun and laughing.

**Laugh! At everything! At yourself!
All the time!**

YOUR CAT IS BEAUTIFUL
... AND KNOWS IT

'Cats never strike a pose that isn't photogenic'

LILIAN JACKSON BRAUN

All cats are beautiful, which is really quite surprising. It is very rare to come across an ugly cat, except if they are never cared for or are old and sick. By definition, a cat is beautiful from birth to death, and suffers little the ravages of time. Do cats get wrinkled? Do cats lose their hair? Why do humans physically degenerate to such an extent? Are we really 'superior' in that regard?

That cats are beautiful isn't at all important in itself. But this confident attitude they have all the time is perhaps conditioned partly by this fact: a cat is beautiful and is maybe conscious of it.

Of course it's possible that a cat has no notion of beauty as regards itself, in which case life is much easier for it. But for us poor humans, beauty is an essential element of our happiness and self-confidence, and we cannot sidestep it with a facile: 'It's the inner beauty that counts.' That's not true, and we all know it.

It's nature's way that we are not all equal in beauty, in that natural grace which some people are simply born with. Still, just because you're not the symbol of an aesthetic ideal doesn't mean you're a vision of ugliness either. There's a huge margin between the two.

And it's this margin which we all must employ in order to feel better in ourselves, a margin to be worked on through our bearing and our clothes. The aim is not to achieve a particular appearance in the eyes of others, but to feel good in yourself and in your wellbeing.

At the end of the day there is only one beauty rule to follow, and only one judge, who is impartial (except if they judge according to codes that are not their own): YOU. You in your mirror. That is all.

If you sincerely think that you're beautiful when you look in the mirror, then your charisma, your aura and consequently your power of seduction will only increase tenfold.

Feeling beautiful is important, if not essential. But you won't get there by following any old criteria.

Wanting to look like a magazine cover – not to mention dubious codes governing thinness or anything else – means not wanting to resemble yourself, and above all not accepting yourself, not loving yourself. Who could ever truly love you through such a masquerade of dissemblance?

You are beautiful for what you are,
and for what you can improve, not for
what is agreed or displayed by others.
Charm is the key.

YOUR CAT'S DAY

11.00: IN THE LAND OF DREAMS

* It's been a long day, tiring even, and it's time to go and count mice ... What better than your thick, soft duvet to soothe away your mental or physical aches and pains? But here comes your cat ... to sleep with you.

* As we saw in 'Cat secrets', it is perhaps not without good reason that your cat comes to snuggle against you or sleep on your belly.

* Have you heard of 'purr therapy'? Or the benefits of a cat who instinctively comes to lie against fatigued or diseased parts of the body? Studies regularly come to light regarding the healing powers of cats. Why not take advantage of them by sleeping with your cat? After all, cats dream of nothing else.

* Having fallen asleep next to your cat, you will often wake in the morning to find it sleeping a little further away in your bed, just to be near you, perhaps at your feet.

* Finally, even if we have lots to learn from cats, we can say that there is one point on which cats resemble humans (whether we're a man or a woman), as illustrated by this Lebanese proverb: 'A cat's dreams are full of mice.'

* Good night.

YOUR CAT IS AT EASE
IN ALL SITUATIONS

*'A gentleman had a favourite cat whom he
taught to sit at the dinner table where it behaved very
well. He was in the habit of putting any
scraps he left onto the cat's plate. One day puss did
not take his place punctually, but presently appeared
with two mice, one of which it placed on its master's
plate, the other on its own'*

THE JOURNAL OF BEATRIX POTTER

It's fair to say that in the course of our lives, there is no lack of situations where we might feel ill at ease, even though, with time, our self-confidence grows and allows us to more easily overcome these delicate situations.

Feeling ill at ease often means feeling that we don't measure up. But who is it we're not measuring up to? Others, of course, and also the image we have of ourselves.

Have you ever seen your cat ill at ease? Never. It's such a human feeling that one simply wouldn't think to attribute it to a cat.

No, your cat will never feel ill at ease in the sense we mean, for as we have seen at various points in this book, your cat has no image to protect: YOUR CAT SIMPLY IS. Consequently, your cat is transparent in its behaviour, and no little fibs about its personality or abilities can shake its confidence or self-esteem.

This feeling of occasional uneasiness is above all down to what we ourselves have constructed, somewhat artificially. Do we run the risk of being 'found out'? Of not measuring up to the stories we've told, the things we've claimed, and everything that makes up the image that others have of us?

We feel ill at ease when we find ourselves up against it, caught between what we have said and what we actually do or are. And the bigger the lies, the bigger the gap between them and the truth, and the greater the feeling of uneasiness. It gives you an idea of the psychological state that mythomaniacs find themselves in when we finally manage to see right through them.

We also feel ill at ease when we feel we don't measure up. This is more an issue of self-confidence, but as we have seen, being sure of yourself and believing in yourself can be cultivated when it doesn't come naturally. And your cat is there to guide you and help you throughout this learning process.

To feel at ease in all situations, you have to be as honest as possible with yourself and with others, and not invest too much in the image you convey to them, for that image can only be a positive one when you follow the ways of your cat.

Always at ease? Not always easy! But it's a victory your cat would be proud of.

YOUR CAT SHOWS EMPATHY

*'When you believe there is no love in the world, look
into the eyes of the cat in your lap'*

OLD WELSH PROVERB

Those who have a cat know this: they will
never refuse to lend an ear. Are we capable of
such altruism? Of such ability to listen? Of such
empathy towards others, as cats are when they look at
us?

We are very much in their shadow when it comes to
empathy, it must be said. Even with the best will in the
world, we sometimes find it difficult to sincerely listen
to others' problems, to put ourselves in their shoes, so
overwhelmed are we by our own issues.

Cats have this innate power, this benevolence
towards us, this sensing of our unease even when we

don't talk to them, and they adopt protective and soothing attitudes towards us.

But beyond the silent listening that a psycho-therapist might provide, cats seem to understand our problems, repeating through their gaze: 'This too shall pass', while filling our emotional emptiness.

We could learn much about empathy and listening from cats, if we could just get past our self-absorption, and reach out our hands and lend our ears to others more than we do.

When we truly listen to others, we give as much as we receive, sometimes without realising.

Learn how to listen in order to be listened to, and learn how to give in order to receive.

FOOD FOR THOUGHT

'A cat has nine lives. For three he plays, for three
he strays and for the last three he stays'

PROVERB

LIVE LIKE A CAT

Most people living with cats envy how they operate, and their inclination to happiness; and they often dream of implementing their cats' behaviours and philosophies in their own everyday lives.

Being able to adopt their approach, and cultivate only that which can bring us serenity, wellbeing, pleasure and fun, and knowing how to rid our lives of everything that weighs us down, without lumbering ourselves with more questions: it sounds like a dream.

Yet it's a dream within reach of us all, as long as we take the time to embrace some of the cat's behaviours as regards our self-esteem, our relationship to others, and our capacity to discern the essential from the futile.

Cats possess an innate knowledge of how to enjoy life to the full, whereas we have much to learn in this area. But there is no lesson to be found in philosophical treatises; cats teach us these things plainly through their way of simply being.

Be inspired by your cat every single day, whether in managing your relationships, channelling your stress, and knowing how to let go and how to rebuild your self-confidence. They are all themes we have tackled through these forty principal abilities that cats have.

They are all keys to enable us to retake possession of a life that sometimes slips from our control.

If you don't have a cat, perhaps you have been surprised to learn that this little ball of fur contains so many abilities and strengths, and so much everyday wisdom. Maybe you will now feel like finding a cat to be your life companion. I hope that you do, for you will never regret the connection that will grow between you both, and the moments and truths you will share together.

And, from now on, live like your cat and make your life a quest for wellbeing and pleasure.

FOOD FOR THOUGHT

'Looking at such an intelligent cat,

I sadly reflect again

on the narrow constraints

of our knowledge.

Who can say where the limits

of these creatures' intellectual

faculties lie?'

ERNST THEODOR AMADEUS HOFFMANN

YOUR CAT ALWAYS HAS THE LAST WORD

My master isn't always the cleverest, and sometimes he can be a real drag. Cat-astrophic, even! But I like him. More than twelve years together now, and I still have my work cut out. For all that, he has made some progress.

I hope that the life lessons he has shared with you will help you to live better in your everyday life, and, above all, be happy.

There are other secrets that I would have liked to convey to him so that he might pass them on to you, but he loses focus sometimes, and doesn't always hear what I'm saying.

But it's all here, right in front of us, in front of you. The difference between you and us cats is that we see everything.

Since Ancient Egyptian times, and even before that, we have been there to help humans. At one time we were venerated for our wisdom, something that tends to be forgotten nowadays.

I hope that this book will be of help to you, so that your vision becomes a little brighter each day.

I wish you all the best and more, dear humans, in your life alongside us.

ZIGGY

TEST

ASSESS YOUR
CAT QUOTIENT (CQ)

For each question, circle the number you
think most accurately reflects you (be honest!).
(From 1 the lowest to 5 the highest)

TEST

1. To what extent do you generally feel free in your life?
   CQ: 1 2 3 4 5

2. Do you think you are very charismatic?
   CQ: 1 2 3 4 5

3. Do you tend to be calm? (Or are you often on edge?)
   CQ: 1 2 3 4 5

4. Are you able to assert yourself, in public and among your nearest and dearest?
   CQ: 1 2 3 4 5

5. Would you say you are a wise person, someone who can see the bigger picture?
   CQ: 1 2 3 4 5

6. Are you able to think about yourself? Can you take care of yourself?
   CQ: 1 2 3 4 5

7. Do you accept yourself as you are, with your qualities and faults? Do you tend to love yourself?
   CQ: 1 2 3 4 5

8. Would you say that you are generally proud, with a high opinion of yourself?
   CQ: 1 2 3 4 5

9. Do you think that you are often the centre of attention?
   CQ: 1 2 3 4 5

10. To what extent are you indifferent to other people's judgements?
    CQ: 1 2 3 4 5

11. Are you curious?
    CQ: 1 2 3 4 5

12. Are you independent?
    CQ: 1 2 3 4 5

13. Do you have confidence in yourself?
    CQ: 1 2 3 4 5

14. Do you know how to delegate?

CQ: 1 2 3 4 5

15. Do you know how to take the time to live and fully enjoy life?

CQ: 1 2 3 4 5

16. Do you adapt easily to change?

CQ: 1 2 3 4 5

17. Do you often seek tranquillity?

CQ: 1 2 3 4 5

18. Would you say that, by and large, you have chosen your friends? (Or have they been imposed on you, or imposed themselves on you?)

CQ: 1 2 3 4 5

19. Do you know how to rest? (Or is that a waste of time as far as you're concerned?)

CQ: 1 2 3 4 5

20. Do you know how to say NO?

CQ: 1 2 3 4 5

21. Do you regularly avoid conflicts?

    CQ: 1 2 3 4 5

22. Are you attached to your living space?

    CQ: 1 2 3 4 5

23. Do you entirely trust your family and friends?

    CQ: 1 2 3 4 5

24. Do you have the soul of a leader?

    CQ: 1 2 3 4 5

25. Are you tenacious? Stubborn? Obstinate?

    CQ: 1 2 3 4 5

26. Are you generally a cautious person?

    CQ: 1 2 3 4 5

27. To what extent do you feel you have a need for
    permanent love?

    CQ: 1 2 3 4 5

28. Do you think you are a serene person?

    CQ: 1 2 3 4 5

29. Are you sure of what you want in life most of the time?

CQ: 1   2   3   4   5

30. Do you regularly dare to ask for help from other people?

CQ: 1   2   3   4   5

31. Do you generally consider yourself to be honest?

CQ: 1   2   3   4   5

32. Do you tend to observe and not say much?

CQ: 1   2   3   4   5

33. Are you faithful in friendship and in your relationships?

CQ: 1   2   3   4   5

34. Are you completely detached from your image, and from material things?

CQ: 1   2   3   4   5

35. Do you consider yourself to be spontaneous and natural?

CQ: 1 2 3 4 5

36. Do you show humility?

CQ: 1 2 3 4 5

37. Do you tend to find amusement in the smallest things?

CQ: 1 2 3 4 5

38. Do you think you're beautiful when you look in the mirror?

CQ: 1 2 3 4 5

39. Do you feel at ease in all situations?

CQ: 1 2 3 4 5

40. Are you capable of listening, and of putting yourself in other people's shoes?

CQ: 1 2 3 4 5

Count your answers:

Number of 1 and 2 answers:

Number of 3 answers:

Number of 4 and 5 answers:

RESULTS OF THE
CAT QUOTIENT TEST

Living like your cat is the Holy Grail for a happy life. But it can require a lot of work for some people.

Look at your results for the
Cat Quotient test:

- If you have a majority of 1 and 2 answers: urgently adopt a cat! Follow them step by step, for they have much to teach you of their behaviours and life philosophy – which will help you to live better.
- If you have a majority of 3 answers: you're a kitten. There is still work to do, but you're on the right path.
- If you have a majority of 4 and 5 answers: Congratulations! You're a cat!

Have a look through the questions again, one by one, and take on board the fact that all those where you answered with less than a 4 may be worthy of your attention, with a view to correcting some of your tendencies and deficiencies – with your cat's help.

These are all abilities, talents and faculties that your cat naturally possesses and which we have analysed throughout this book. Now you only have to calmly integrate them into your life for a serene existence.